# Ali and Sonni

By Adriana Diaz-Donoso

Library For All Ltd.

Ali and Sonni

This edition published 2022

Published by Library For All Ltd
Email: info@libraryforall.org
URL: libraryforall.org

Library For All gratefully acknowledges the contributions of all who made previous editions of this book possible.

Ali and Sonni
Diaz-Donoso, Adriana
ISBN: 978-1-922827-78-4
SKU02673

# Ali and Sonni

Ali and Sonni love fruit and vegetables, and they like to eat them fresh.

One day, Sonni got sick.

She had a fever and felt extremely weak.

Her mum was worried and took her to the doctor.

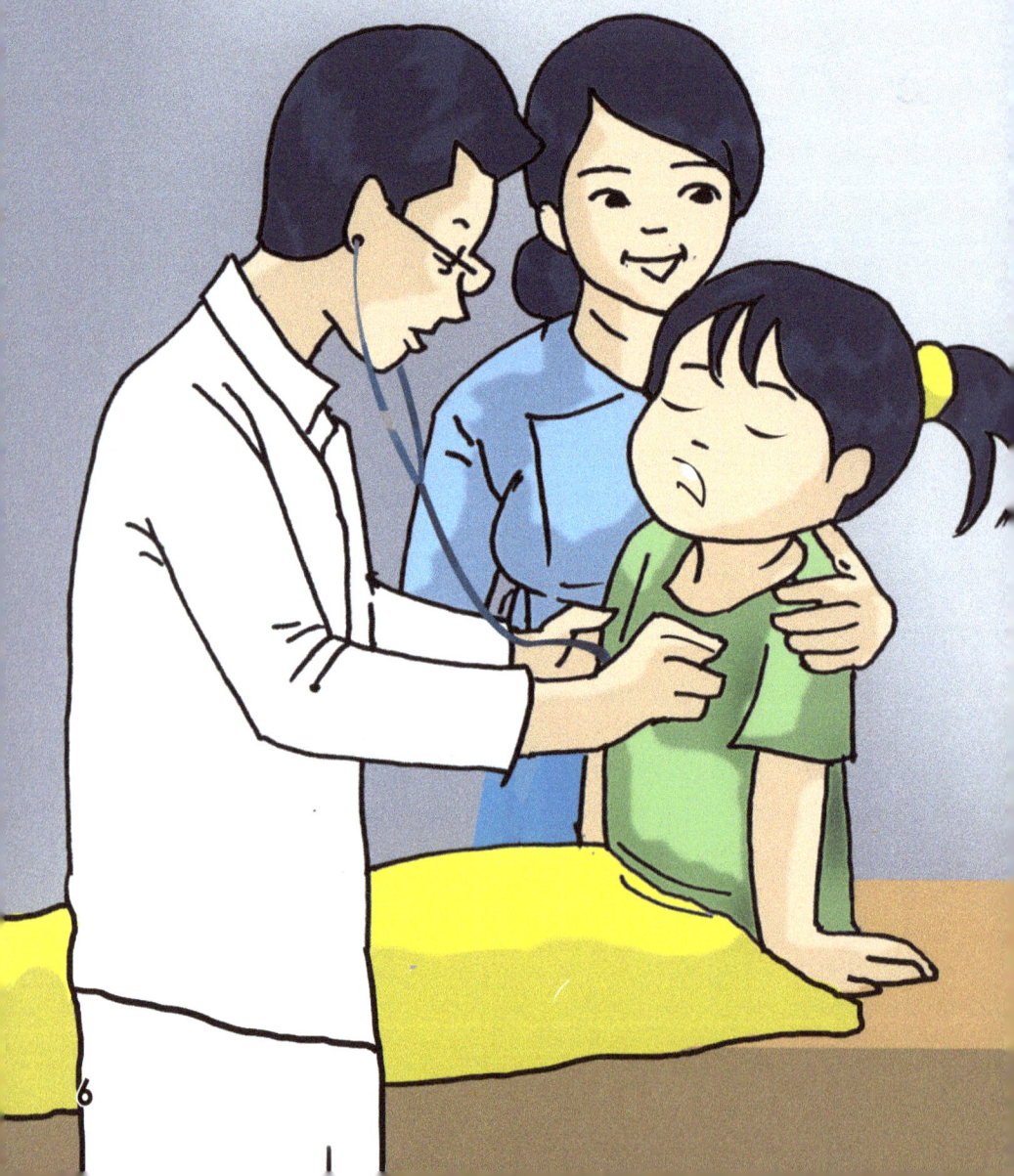

The doctor said that
a worm was making
her sick.

So he gave her a
de-worming drug
to kill it.

Back home, Sonni felt better but did not know why this terrible worm was living inside her because she always wears shoes to play with her friends.

She also urinates and defecates in a toilet.

And she always washes her hands after.

She could not stop
thinking about it and
asked her friend Ali
for help.

He said, "Did you
remember to wash the
delicious fruit you like
to eat with clean water?"

Sonni replied, "Oh no! I always forget to wash them. I love fruit so much and they just look so tasty, I end up eating them before I remember to wash them."

"I will definitely wash my fruit with clean water every time before eating because, like you, I love to eat fruit, but I don't want to get sick again!" said Sonni.

# You can use these questions to talk about this book with your family, friends and teachers.

What did you learn from this book?

Describe this book in one word. Funny? Scary? Colourful? Interesting?

How did this book make you feel when you finished reading it?

What was your favourite part of this book?

download our reader app
getlibraryforall.org

# About the contributors

Library For All works with authors and illustrators from around the world to develop diverse, relevant, high quality stories for young readers. Visit libraryforall.org for the latest news on writers' workshop events, submission guidelines and other creative opportunities.

# Did you enjoy this book?

We have hundreds more expertly curated original stories to choose from.

We work in partnership with authors, educators, cultural advisors, governments and NGOs to bring the joy of reading to children everywhere.

# Did you know?

We create global impact in these fields by embracing the United Nations Sustainable Development Goals.

libraryforall.org